Welcome to the story of the Glastonbury Dragons

The Glastonbury Dragons have been sleeping under Glastonbury Tor for quite a long time.

But now they were stirring and starting to waken.

They needed new heads and bodies to be seen.

So they called out to someone to make them again.

Yuri and Steve heard their call.

Yuri asked Steve to help make the Dragons.

Steve who is the Dragon Master created them and Yuri painted them.

So people could see them once again.

This is the story of how the Glastonbury Dragons 2016 were created

The beginning of the Dragons was all made outside from tent poles and other metal.

The weather sometimes stopped work because it was cold and raining.

So The Dragon Master's parents gave him a gazebo which meant work could continue through rain and sunshine.

The Dragon heads started to appear.

Yuri painted the Red Dragon head.

Greg sat inside while Steve taped the Dragons.

Yuri then tested the Red Dragon head to see if he can carry it.

He can, it is light and easy to hold.

The Red Dragon is now having skirting put on it by Steve, the Dragon Master.

Greg is sitting inside to hold the Dragon up.

The White Dragon has been created by Steve, The Dragon Master.

Now it is the White Dragons turn to be painted.

Can you see the foam rolls that will make up the skirt?

There is paint all over the ground, glue everywhere, rolls of foam and all sorts around.

But the White Dragon was starting to take shape.

The Red and White Dragons are nearly ready.

The Dragons just need their bodies making now.

These are made from red material and white material plus lots of hoops.

The material is sown and the hoops put in place.

Look at the Red Dragon, waiting to go to practice.

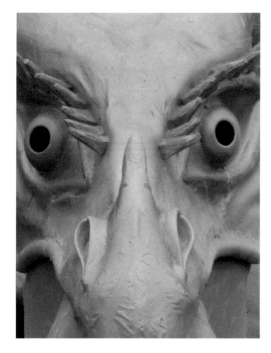

And the White Dragon, waiting to go to practice.

A couple of Dragon Practices were held in the local car park. The Dragons were 'test driven'.

Everything worked. The Dragons were now ready to go to the Beltane Glastonbury Dragons Celebrations.

First the Red Dragon emerged into the waiting crowd.

And then the White Dragon came a while later.

The Glastonbury Dragons meet in public for the very first time. The crowd loved them, they seemed to raise the energy.

Children wanted to keep touching the Dragons noses!

Lots of people came to celebrate May Day and to see the new Dragons.

Some people dressed up for the occasion.

The Dragons have banners, one for the Red Dragon and one for the White Dragon.

The banners were made and painted by Yuri.

The Red Dragon, with the White Dragon Banner, in Glastonbury Market Place.

The Dragons also have Drummers who walk with them.

The drum beat helps the Dragons to find their way.

The Dragons have people inside them so they can move.

These people are called Dragons Legs.

The Glastonbury Dragons have returned.

Glastonbury Beltane 2016 – Dragons return

They had a good time but are now resting until October when they will return for Samhain.

Yuri created this logo for the Dragons.

It is now October and time for the Dragons to emerge again.

GLASTONBURY DRAGONS
CELEBRATIONS
PRESENTS...

... ITS FIRST...

SAMHAIN
WILD
HUNT !

SATURDAY 29TH OCTOBER

A TWILIGHT FIRE & LANTERN FESTIVAL

The Dragons have now rested.

They have also had more paint put on them.

Can you spot the difference?

It is October and the time of Samhain.

The Dragons are excited, they are walking to meet people again.

The Drummers lead the Dragons with the drum beat.

People follow the Dragons.

Can you see the Red Dragon's tail?

The White Dragon walks along to the Chalice Well.

The Red Dragon follows.

Can you see the Dragons legs?

Lots of people walk with the Dragons.

Can you see the drummers?

The Red and White Dragons stay at the Chalice Well for a short while.

They are waiting to go home.

The Dragons are happy, they have emerged and been seen again.

But for now they are sleeping.

Watch out for them emerging again in May.